When I was a girl, I had dreams about being a mum. I imagined what life would be like when I grew up, got married and had children – just like my mum did.

I was lucky enough to come from a stable family with good foundations. It was a typical family: Mum and Dad both worked, and we all lived in the same house. We were not rich but I knew for certain that we were not poor. Far from it.

This created certain ideals in my head. I was going to marry a man who was older than me, taller than me, earned more than I did and who came from a "reputable" family like ours.

It was drummed into my subconscious how "well-brought up" we were going to be whether we liked it or not. There were things we didn't do, things we must do and things that were not to be talked about. We were being brought up to be model citizens who did well in school; prioritised education; went to church; had the right manners and looked right- always.

We were brought up to be survivors, leaders, public speakers, and people of note. We were examples of how kids should be, we complied, mostly. We were never really in serious trouble. Never really brought shame to the family- apart from when my parents came to get me from a pool party at age 16. It was a party for two of my friends. It was arranged by their respectable parents- who worked in the respectable university like mine and came from respectable households like we did. I am still not sure why they had to come and drag me out in front of all my friends, I digress.

I grew up with the false notion that it would be easy to bring up children to comply with my values and they would fall in line with every plan I had for them.

I did not know I would struggle with the most inane things! And my children are not even teenagers yet. For instance, when do I tell my daughters that their dad was not my first husband? How do I handle the fact that they already have questions about being mixed race? How do I explain that having two daughters and no son is not a health condition? How do I explain that it is for their own good that I stopped them from visiting a friend who never visited them back?

I am no expert in anything to do with parenting. All I know is that I have lived it. I am bringing up two daughters who are under six now and already, I have many triumphs but also many pitfalls. I cannot be the only one walking this road, so here are my tips on surviving young daughters.

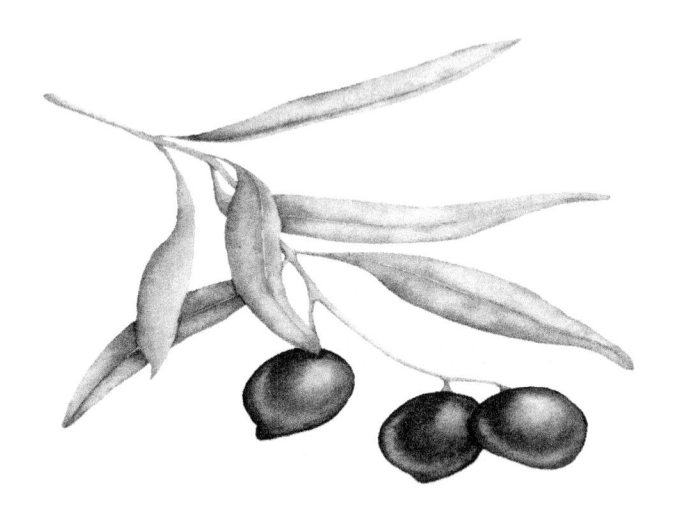

Food

I stopped breastfeeding my younger daughter who is now two years old when she was 12 months old. That was the plan. What I did not prepare for, was the fact that she would then detest any kind of milk and hence my plan for ensuring her nutrition, going forward.

Both had things they just refused to eat. They both went through periods where I feared they'd die of malnutrition and or starvation. I had some meltdowns of my own over their feeding. There were times it seemed like they were not eating at all.

It was not part of the plan to have children who were fussy eaters! I was "training" them to appreciate a varied diet... that is what I wanted to be able to say! I wanted to be able to declare that "Zara just eats whatever I put on her plate" or that "Xanthe just loves her broccoli".

The truth is that no one gets a medal for how early they started loving vegetables. Even if they did get a medal, how boring must life be for anyone who focuses on that.

For children who come from loving families, as long as there is food in the house, those children cannot and will not die of starvation.

They will be little brats about their feeding and your plans for their nutrition, but that lasts until you find a way or until they learn that hunger is not pleasant. It is easy for me to say that you shouldn't stress about it but take it from someone who has walked that mile. Do not STRESS!

Trust your instincts. I realised that one of my daughters loved anything in a fancy cup with a straw. So I got a cup with a straw and blended some avocados, cashew nuts, spinach, yoghurt and honey. Even I, loved it! And I was sure she was getting some food that way. It was practically a balanced diet in a cup, and she didn't even realise she had been outsmarted. We had variations of this "drink" daily and my mind was more at ease, until she decided she no longer liked it. Back to the drawing board. (

Please, make sure your ingredients are age appropriate).

One thing that a dear friend said to me when my baby didn't seem to want any food at what I thought her feeding times should be, was this: Let her lead.

That statement switched my mind on, and I got it. Why am I insisting that she eats now? For a baby who can't talk, the best form of communication is to take cues from their body language and let them lead. Don't force them into what you think is an ideal schedule.

Let them show you what their ideal is. That simple statement was a game changer for me.

For children of school age, however, I still have my ideal values that I would like them to conform to. I would like for them to appreciate the effort I have made to get food on their plates. Especially if I have cooked rather than just thrown some chips and chicken nuggets in the oven. I would like them to sit and use their cutlery and table manners and eat everything on their plates. Whilst I realise that this could be wishful thinking, there are elements of that that I believe are important in character building. I want them to learn gratitude for even what may seem small. I want them to learn to show appreciation for efforts made for them- in any sphere of life; I believe that it is important that they understand that even though food is not a privilege, they are better off than some, having the type of food that they have. I want them to be adaptable and make do with what has been provided rather than demand an alternative.

So for the reasons above, as they grow older, I will insist more that they devour anything I cook with relish! I will push back more on them preferring something other than what I have provided. I will make sure that there are consequences for their lack of gratitude and respect around food. All within reason , of course.

Someone once told me that children of all ages tend to use food as control mechanism. I am not sure I fully understand that. They tried to explain that as children grow, they start to use food to manipulate your mood and responses. Again, I sort of see how that could happen, but I don't know how I feel about toddlers having the sense to manipulate anything. But with that in mind, I would suggest that as much as you can, don't let food become "a thing."

Let them not see any emotion rise from you as a result of their attitude towards food. Especially if it is a negative emotion, an anxious emotion, a confused emotion... you get the picture? Don't let it become a thing. Maybe it is one of the occasions where you either let them lead or you let them see that the consequence of not eating what was provided, is hunger. "Darling, you don't want to eat your food? *Oh, that's ok. Just put it to the side, it will be there when you are ready. I can't feed you anything else until you have tried what I made for you*".

Zara would devour whatever was placed on her plate as long as it is in a restaurant or café. Xanthe started doing the same. I took it to heart at first and started to internalise as I do. I started to feel inadequate as a mother. There is this whole thing of people saying their mums are the best cook in the world. I don't know if it is an African thing. But in my case, my mother is actually the best cook in the world. I have never aspired to be the best cook, but I expect that as a bare minimum, my children eat what I cook.

But as I said, don't let food become a thing. Their loving of restaurant food is not a reflection of my cooking. It is "a nothing." They like new places to eat. Who doesn't?

I can't even begin to tell you the pleasant and not so pleasant surprises when it came to my native food.

Tantrums

My biggest tip with regard to tantrums is that you should resign yourself to the fact that they will happen.

Have a strategy for when they happen but know that your strategy may be completely useless in the heat of the moment.

What you should prepare for is your emotional state. If you are resigned to tantrums taking place, then you will not fall to pieces along with your child when they are going on. Also, you will not stress about how it looks in public when your kid is kicking off and making it look like social services should be involved.

There are different types of tantrums and different reasons for them. The terrible twos is a thing. But it starts before they are two and never really completely ends.

The thing is, you know your child better than anyone. No one can tell you the best way to handle your child's tantrum. For me, distraction seemed to work a lot. Just suddenly showing over enthusiastic interest in anything would sometimes make them pause and perhaps forget the reason they were screaming the place down.

Sometimes, I used the firm voice method and it worked. Other times, it made them scream even louder. Sometimes, I let it ride out and other times, I held them tight and reassured them.

What matters is that you get to know your child and through trial and error, you will learn the signs and know what kind of response Is most effective. Don't make the tantrum about you. It is not about how it makes you look; it is not about what kind of parent you are. It is a tantrum. Kids do it.

Never lose control. They depend on you to be emotionally intelligent enough to deal with their meltdowns. No matter how escalated it may seem, please try to hold your nerve and fall apart later- when they can't witness it.

A word for the parents who have died several times over because their child has decided to have a meltdown in public. It is ok. In the heat of the moment it is hard to think straight because you are putting up a performance of your own for the people witnessing your child go ballistic. You are losing your nerve and composure because you can't remember the script to your own performance. Remember, your child having a tantrum is not about any of those other people you are imploring with your eyes not to judge you. Your child having a tantrum is another opportunity for you to parent. Compose yourself and decide how best to address YOUR CHILD – not anyone else.

In my opinion, a toddler tantrum is different from a baby who just cries and cries and cries and cries. I remember taking Xanthe to the hospital because she would not stop crying. She must have been about 3 months old. The doctor examined her and heard what we had to say and diagnosed her with "crying baby syndrome" for which there is no cure (this is where I insert the emoji for hopelessness- if there was one). I nearly burst into tears myself. I was almost wishing they would tell me something was wrong with her so I could fix it.

After the initial despair of not knowing how to soothe my baby when she decided to properly exercise her lungs, I learned to cope with it. I ensured that she was fed and clean. Made sure there was nothing I should have done that was left undone where she was concerned, then I sat back and let her cry to her heart's content while I held her and made sure she knew that I was there.

I am not an advocate for the thing where they let the baby cry and self soothe. I tried it and lasted about a minute at the longest. It may work for people. It did not work for me. I did not want my very small baby crying till she was too tired to cry anymore . I could not sit back and let my small baby weep herself to sleep. I just couldn't do it. So, I had to be giving myself perspective. As stressful as that period of life was, it was a very very short season in my daughter's life. Soon she would be able to communicate and I would be able to help her process whatever it is that made her cry.

While I disagree with controlled crying in babies, in little girls aged three and over, especially those ones who can talk, I have no problems in letting them cry a little bit. But if the crying is as a result of consequences of their actions. I believe that children should have age appropriate discipline and sometimes, crying is part of that.

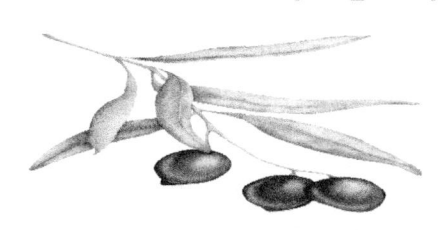

Discipline

This is always a bone of contention. Isn't it? Should you discipline a child? How should you discipline a child? I am not here to tell any parent how to help their child navigate through right and wrong choices.

I am here to say parents SHOULD help their children navigate through right and wrong choices.

I am of African descent and I live in the UK. So I have seen how both cultures approach the issue of discipline.

Your children should have a healthy dose of fear. They should know why it is wrong to do somethings. They should understand that some actions come with consequences. I am not saying your children should be afraid of you. I have seen many families where as soon as they hear daddy or mummy's car parking up in the drive, everyone scampers into hiding because daddy or mummy's coming back makes the atmosphere tense. Their presence makes everyone walk on eggshells.

There is an African Proverb that goes along the lines of: "*while you correct a child with your left hand, you should embrace him with the right*"

There are times I have exaggerated the extent of the wrongdoing because I want to scare them off doing it ever again. One time, I let Zara visit a friend and apparently, she had told her friend's mum a little white lie. She was four years old. I don't even remember what the lie was. It was something cute that the lady was laughing about while she was telling me. I smiled but gave Zara "the look". She knew what that look meant. When we got in the car, I told her she was in huge trouble for telling lies. I know that I frightened her for what seemed like a petty offence. But those are the kind of things that I don't want to overlook. I don't want the little cute white lies to evolve unchecked. So my punishment and scolding, would have seemed over the top to someone who was not part of our family. But we have values that we want to uphold and there are somethings that must be nipped in the bud.

There are times that I scold my kids and or punish them, I look at them and feel so sorry for them. I don't want to see them cry. I don't want to be the reason they cry, but at the same time, I don't want my lack of action now, to cost them in the future.

As they grow older, and I ensure that they know I am on their side and that they can talk to me about anything, the need to discipline them becomes less and less. I am not deluded though. I know the teenage years are coming. However, I am making hay while the sun shines. I am feeding them shovels full of our family values and I am making sure our relationship is sturdy enough to weather the coming years. I am, to an extent, magnifying the consequences now so that they continue to have a childlike but healthy fear of wrong choices.

I hope I do not come across as someone who revels in punishing her kids, or someone who is obsessed with their right or wrong actions. I am definitely one of those parents who wants her kids to be the best behaved everywhere.

Because those were the expectations placed on me. but honestly, who doesn't want their kids to be one of the best.

The truth is, my main focus is who they grow up into. I have observed parents in western culture and parents in African culture. The ideal situation is somewhere in the middle. Parents in Africa are very protective of the family name and reputation. So there is a tight leash on kids and perhaps not enough room for them to learn from their own mistakes. There is a pressure that I deem unnecessary for children and families to outdo one another. Families end up living their lives according to public opinion.

In the West, children are given room to make too many mistakes. They are allowed to grow up too quickly and their parents become peers rather than remain standards of authority.

So, don't be too harsh with the discipline. Don't overdo it. The reason for discipline is not to hurt your child but to correct them.

If you are genuinely correcting them and it brings some tears, that is no reason to leave bad behaviour unchecked.

While it is good to be a strict parent, do not be a tyrant. While it is good to be your child's "friend", do not forget to parent. Emotionally and morally, your children need a compass.

Children also need to learn how to be accountable. I can sometimes tell what an adult's childhood was like. Sometimes you come across adults who don't answer to anyone. They have no one in their lives that they will humbly listen to. They are a law unto themselves and cannot handle being accountable to anyone.

I see them as people who were not loved enough to be corrected. People whose parents couldn't be bothered enough to raise responsible adults.

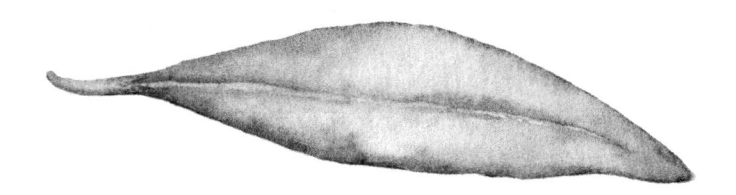

Identity

When I was growing up, there were clear cut roles for males and females. The man was the head of the family and if a woman was wise, she would be the neck that coyly turned the head in the direction that she wanted to steer the family.

In my culture, even today, the male child is favoured. You could heave a sigh of relief once you gave birth to a boy.

So with that at the back of my head, I always assumed I would be blessed with a boy and a girl. If I got two boys, that would be absolutely fine.

So imagine me now with two daughters. We had a neighbour who had nine daughters and child number 10 was a boy... phew!

I live in the UK and my children are half white British. So the pressure is less. I remember going to Nigeria while pregnant with my second child and thanking God I hadn't as of that time, found out the sex of the baby. Everyone wanted to know. I could feel their angst as they asked me if I knew if it was male or female. I am not complaining. It is the way we have been conditioned.

So now, as a black woman, a black woman who is in touch with her African culture, not having a son, brings with it a huge responsibility of changing age-old notions that girls are less than boys.

It is not a task I signed up for but one that I will not shirk away from.

Another dynamic to add to the list is that we are a multi-cultural and multi-racial family. We live in a part of England that is a bit low on the diversity quota. So while I have had to cope with being the only one or one of the few black women in most of the spaces I find myself, already, I see the impact of skin colour on my children.

My daughter once told me, at age four that she had to play by herself in school because she was told by another kid that "NO BLACK GIRLS ALLOWED" in the playhouse. Ooh! I can feel my blood pressure rising just by remembering that incident.

I knew it was coming, I just didn't think it was coming so soon. I had made sure that her identity was not whitewashed. For world book day, she had gone to school as Queen Amina and for the year after that, she went as Shuri- The Black Panther's sister. I made sure she knew she had black girl magic. She had been to Nigeria three times already!

So imagine my shock when at age five she makes the following comments at different times:

- *Mummy, I hope I get lighter when I grow up.*
- *I don't really like dark skin*

- *When pink men (she referred to white people as pink- I have not corrected it yet. I don't need to) can't find pink women to marry, they say "ok, I will just have a brown one"*
- *I don't like my afro.*

All my hard work to make sure this girl was proud of who she is and she comes out with statements like that at ages four and five. I always tell parents not to fall to pieces in front of their children and not to exhibit emotions that tell you have lost control in front of your child.

Well, I broke those rules at each of those events.

I lost control, either ugly cried in front of my poor daughter or lectured her for weeks and just as we were settling into the rhythm, she would drop another one of those clangers.

I know the issues of identity are not all about race. There are questions of class, sexuality, gender identity, disability, religion, culture and so on. Every family has that thing they believe sets them apart or that thing that is their main identity. It is a fantastic thing to have that thing that identifies you or that you use to identify yourselves as a unit.

When I was growing up, it was the fact that my parents were from different tribes. Then it became this motto that my dad created "*Ihemes NEVER FAIL*". I loved it. I loved it as long as I was not failing. It helped with my confidence and it motivated me. and when I was failing, it helped get me to sit up. But when I was failing and there was no hope... like in my first marriage, it was like a stone around my leg and I was drowning in the ocean.

Luckily, I had parents who were emotionally intelligent enough to know when to use my identity to add pressure and when to ease off. Well, they mostly knew- they didn't always get it right.

So each time my five year old deviated from her identity or scorned it or just act toward it like a five year old would, I struggled. No idea if this is when I should be emphasising her identity or this is when I should shut up about it and not use it to mount undue pressure. I struggled because I wondered if it was my emphasising her identity as a mixed-race black girl that caused her to shun it sometimes. I had no idea why she would make comments like that. Where was it coming from?

It was the same thing when she first started going to nursery. Her father was adamant that he did not want her sounding a certain way. She was picking up this accent that was not in line with the class he associated himself with. His parents were very class conscious and cared a lot about how they came across and how their children presented. My family was the same. So he was forever correcting her when she would say "shlaaiid" instead of "slide". I found it funny. That was not the aspect of her identity I was concerned with.

So what to do when your child deviates from who you want them to be at age five?

I will give you another quick example. One day, we went to the beach. I was pregnant with my second child. We got there and we started to build sandcastles with Zara. A little girl and her brother approached us and we let them join us. Their parents waved at us and it was ok to let them play with Zara and us as we were building these sandcastles. Zara was two years old and it was going well.

The girl was five and her brother was three. She was so well spoken she even intimidated me. Her accent was how we thought our kid should sound and this was around the time that my husband was battling Zara's seemingly crass tone.

The little girl built six castles and made them really pretty while she chatted away in her lovely voice and accent. Being ever so well behaved and telling us about her family and how her aunty was visiting from America and how her mother was such a clever lady blah blah blah when suddenly my kid becomes a little thug and stamps on all six sandcastles in her deep less than favourable accent and sudden brutish behaviour!

I was horrified!

How do you handle your child deviating from who you would like them to be? I am not after one of those answers about how you cannot decide who your child is and let them be their own person etc etc .....Not that.

I am talking about values that matter to you. The kind of behaviour that goes against your core aspirations for your child and family. Behaviour that you cannot and should not ignore?

This sounds too deep a conversation to have when the

child in question is only five years old. But it is the reality. The world in which we live is such that there are so many extraneous factors that influence our kids and if we are not careful, our voices will be drowned out by the volume of everything else.

I have not found the answer. I do not know the solution. It is a constant battle. One thing I can vouch for, is the power of repetition. A continuous reminding of who we are, how we are, a continuous search for opportunities to celebrate, glamorise and emphasize the aspects of our identity that we do not want our children to deviate from. And one day, they will make comments or do things that show us that the message is sinking in.

It is in things like this that I have admiration for children who come from minority families. So where I live, in the UK, I have admiration for Sikh families when I see their children bounding around in a turban or head covering. I know what battles the parents have overcome to get their children to accept that vital part of their identity. I see the children- especially the teenagers who join their Jehovah's witnesses' parents to go house to house and I have a new respect for those parents.

So I suppose my main tip is that be prepared to be one of the voices that influence your child. You have a unique opportunity to be the loudest voice in their lives. And I don't mean loudest shouty voice, I mean loudest influencing voice. Perseverance is key. Remember who we are is not just about what we do; it is in every aspect of our lives. So be the example you want your kids to emulate.

Children asking questions and challenging things is to be expected. It is a sign of intelligence and critical thinking. Be honest with them and transparent. If there are answers you don't have, let them know that you don't have the answers. Don't get defensive- it is off putting.

Another story for you:

When I was a kid, I believed I was the most beautiful girl in my nursery. I genuinely believed this.

Right up to around age 10. I had no doubt in my mind whatsoever that I was absolutely gorgeous. When I look at childhood pictures now, I just laugh. I was not the most beautiful at all!

I was gangly, looked like a boy and was just strange looking. I am lucky that I was completely unaware of that fact that I was not even cute. My self esteem would have been non-existent.

Do you know why I thought I was the most beautiful girl? You guessed. I heard it from home.

Somehow, my parents were able to be loud enough in my mind and my psyche to convince me to carry myself like the most beautiful girl.

I remind myself of this every time now. When Zara makes one of those comments about her identity, I remind myself that if my father and mother could get me to think I was the most beautiful girl on the planet, then I can make Zara realise how beautiful and special she is. I can get her to fully accept and love who she is.

Don't be the silent voice in your child's life.

Parental Rivalry

This is one of those of ones. (this one warrants the side eye emoji).

Forgive my generalisation with this one and the stereotype, but I think many mums will get this. I am not sure how it works in families with two mums or two dads.

But as a mum, I seem to be the visionary where the kids are concerned. I seem to be the one who is pushing more for the girls to have a bit of "magic" in their lives.- the fairytales, Father Christmas, the toys that their dad would initially deem unnecessary…, the trips to places like the aquarium. Those kind of things that their dad would say "it is cheaper to watch the fish on TV than it is to visit the aquarium; why don't we watch wildlife on TV instead of spending that amount of money going to the zoo?". It is me who agonises over what school I want them to attend. It is me that makes sure they are dressed well and don't look homeless…

But it is also me that watches how much they adore their daddy! They are very much daddy's girls. It is me who captures the beautiful moments on camera. I remember telling Simon that the girls may grow up believing he was a single dad because all the pictures are of his magical moments with them and there were none of me doing anything nice with them. No moments captured, only pictures where I look like a whale and not the yummy mummy I hope I am.

When I was a young girl, I was daddy's girl too! Now as a mum myself, I see that my mum would have pulled most of the strings for us to have the childhood that we did. But my dad was my hero. Only now do I see how they played their complementary roles so brilliantly well.

Recently, I was home with Zara. I was working from home and she had been sent home from school because she was not well. It was ME who was able to drop everything and get her from school and bring her home, nurse her and try to cheer her up. I noticed she was a bit down after a couple of hours so I went to sit next to her for a cuddle and asked what the problem was.

Get ready for another side eye emoji. The problem was that she was missing her daddy! She even proceeded to make the following statement "I have daddy on my heart and I miss him... (droopy mouth, sad eyes, whiny voice)". How did I respond? "Rolled my eyes... Zara that doesn't even make sense! What are you missing him for? He is only at work! Get a grip!"

I know, I should be ashamed.

However, she was saying this in a period that was difficult for her dad and I. Our relationship had been strained over the last few days and it was on thin ice. So, every soppy daddy's girl recital was not going to get a positive response from me.

I usually love it when my girls idolise their daddy. I love watching them bond. I am endlessly telling tales about how they have some of their daddy's characteristics and how they just look so much like him! I love the "oh look at Xanthe as a baby, she is just Simon's double". I love all that until Simon and I are not in good terms.

When our relationship is strained, I am ashamed to admit that it hurts when they run to him rather than me; or when they miss him, or when they want him to do the bedtime story and not me.

Don't get me wrong. They love me too. And there are several times they want their mummy. It is just that sometimes, they want daddy too.

I worked for the organisation that administers child support in the UK. I had this job before I got married and had children. I saw how women used their children as weapons. They used access to the kids as rewards or penalties for the other parent acting in accordance with their will. It is wrong. I have seen parents actively poison their kids against the other parent.

As difficult as it is, as long as the relationship between them and their other parent is not abusive, it should be encouraged. We don't want our children to feel torn, conflicted and confused. Whether we like to admit it or not, having two parents who love them brings more stability and security than having just one.

In the meantime, remember what I said about repetition and being the voice of influence in your child's life? Do that.

I never witnessed my parents have a row till I was a teenager. Now I know how difficult that must have been to shield us from their conflict. Even as a teenager when I did see them have a disagreement, I cannot explain the turmoil I felt.

I have not been able to keep disputes between their father and I away from them. I kick myself every time we let it escalate in front of them. I am scared that I am damaging my kids. That I am scarring them for life or teaching them that it is normal to lose control in a relationship. I don't want them growing up and only being able to function in a relationship where there is drama.

So my tip is, if you are not always able to keep your strife and disagreements away from the children, then let them see that although conflict may occur, things don't remain that way. Let them witness your conflict management skills. It is important they know that your conflict is resolved and not brushed under the carpet. Every time you are careless enough to let them see you at loggerheads, you must be careful enough to ensure that they see you resolve it. Pretend if you must- for your child's sake.

Another quick tip: when they ask for something, if their other parent has previously said no to their request, don't overrule their decision without checking with them first. Presenting a united front is more important than your need to make a point or your need to be good cop.

Always apply common sense of course.

Sibling Rivalry

As the oldest child of three, let me tell you something you may not have thought of. The younger children have the benefit of my hindsight. So naturally, they should do better than I did.

It does not make me less capable than they are; It does not mean that I am a bit thick; it does not mean that they are naturally better at stuff. No. it is just that they have benefited from my hindsight. Even in the most minor stuff.

I remember that as a young child, many relatives and family friends praised my younger brother and sister and did it in a way that caused me to feel like I was a bit stupid.

Currently, Zara is learning to skateboard (oh the drama!) she has been learning to skateboard for a couple of years. Xanthe who is only two years old, seems to have more of a knack for it. The same with ballet. Xanthe has sat and watched Zara at her ballet class for two years. Now that Xanthe is old enough to join the class, she seems to take to ballet like a duck to water. I hear their dad and others praise Xanthe- which is fantastic. However, they praise Xanthe to the detriment of Zara. I hear how they now use Xanthe as the yardstick for Zara to follow. "Zara, can't you see how your sister just does it?" "Zara, Xanthe will soon be better at it than you are".

Luckily, because I am the eldest child and I remember how those innocent statements made me feel, I am on hand to be the louder voice in Zara's head.

Despite my efforts, I see that if left unchecked, Zara could become a bit mean to her sister. As it stands, she is there to highlight every little wrong thing her sister does. I don't want that for my children. I want them to be a team. I don't want people to accidently cause them to become rivals where they are constantly trying to outdo each other.

Xanthe will always have the benefit of Zara's hindsight, but Zara is the one paving the way. She is the one who is in unchartered territory.

It goes the other way too. Zara was born very premature. I was only 27 weeks pregnant. It was a difficult time because we were in hospital for a long time. She came on oxygen. So we built her confidence by telling her what she overcame as a baby. We built her superhero persona.

Xanthe's birth was like going to the dentist. In and out of hospital in about 24 hours. So we have not had cause to build her up as a superhero. She gets the dregs of Zara's "super heroness". Xanthe is delicate and slight in her build. She is cute. So we emphasize her prettiness and Zara's sturdiness. At their tender ages, they may not understand that. Especially if the narrative is that Zara is not as pretty as Xanthe and Xanthe is not as strong as Zara.

Of course, every human being has strengths and weaknesses. And I am all for a bit of healthy competition. All I am saying is be a bit more aware of your language when you praise or criticise. Remember the ages of the kids and try to be mindful of how it may come across to them.

To clarify, I am not one of those mums who believes a medal should be given for simply turning up. I am not one of those "*everybody is a winner*" mums. I am just mentioning it so that perhaps you will catch yourself next time you are praising one child to the detriment of the other.

My daughters are being told that they have no choice but to be each other's best friend. I remember a severe telling off I got when I was about six. I had scolded my younger brother because he upset my friend. Woah! My mother went for it. I was NEVER to take sides with anyone against my brother- no matter what!

I have seen close hand how sibling rivalry has been left to fester until adulthood. It is sad. I have seen how one sibling's perception has been left unchecked and has evolved over the years to bind that person in insecurity and inferiority/superiority complex.

(side note: in my opinion, inferiority and superiority complexes are the same thing).

I make myself laugh when my kids disagree and sometimes, the punishment is to sit on the steps and hug each other for a few minutes.

I am no expert parent. I am just one who has observed human beings and seen that a lot could have been fixed earlier on in their lives.

Ill Health.

This is the worst. We spent nine weeks in hospital when Zara was born. She was three months premature and seeing her 1lb 13oz body in that incubator for that long pulled me in all sorts of directions.

At that age, with the severity of what was going on, I got to know myself. That was introduction to motherhood, and it was brutal.

Fast forward a few years. We were in the supermarket, Zara was two.

From nowhere, she starts to projectile vomit. Oh my days! I am glad to say that I am a good actress and I my total confusion and fear was not expressed at all. Her father on the other hand... (crying laughing emoji). He made a funny sound each time she threw up and was frozen as we watched a small pool of vomit form at her feet.

The staff swung into action and helped out.

Because she was not in pain and she seemed ok in herself, I could reassure her that she would be ok.

It is a different story when they are in pain or discomfort. Xanthe went floppy on us and we had to rush to the hospital. I was scared. But could not let Zara know that I was scared. Like I keep saying, it is ok to show emotion but please don't lose control. Cry if you want to, but don't let your child lose hope. It is damaging.

I am not sure why I have added this heading to be honest. We never know how we would react in situations where our minds are telling us that the most precious things to us are hanging in a balance.

As an eight-year-old, I broke my leg. Twice, I was in hospital a few hours away from home for three months. I never saw my parents cry. The circumstances were very difficult. It was during religious riots where many people were slaughtered. It was at a time when we were hiding in a family friend's house for safety. I went and did the most inconvenient thing of breaking my leg.

The details of that story are for another day. But what I am trying to say is that if that happened to one of my children, I would totally lose it.

But my parents. I never saw them fall pieces over it. Therefore, I didn't feel fear over that situation. I felt the physical pain of the broken leg. But no angst and no fear for the wider situation.

Now, I know how they felt. I know the weight of the decisions they had to make. But they shielded me.

I want to do that for children. I don't want the opportunity to present itself where I have to reassure them over serious health situations. But should it happen, I don't want to give them fear instead of faith.

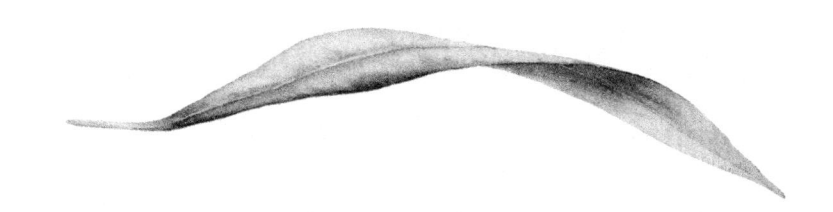

Competition

It is natural for human beings to compete. It is the way we are wired. It must be something to do with the survival of the fittest thing.

But there are some parents who take it too far. I remember being on a Facebook group for The Game of Thrones. It was during the last season and everyone was commenting on the series and we were feeling a bit sad that it was ending. One woman posted quite a detailed drawing of a dragon. It was really nice and well done. She made the mistake of claiming it was done by her four year old. Oh boy!! She was slaughtered online. I know there can be gifted children, but this was too blatant a lie! Oh her four year old had also written "Dracarys" under this drawing of hers. (Google it. Game of Thrones fans will understand Dracarys). That made her lie a bit too much for people to ignore. She didn't think it through. First of all, how does a four-year-old know what Dracarys is? Why are you letting your child watch Game of Thrones? I would be reluctant to let anyone under 18 watch such a TV series. There were too many questions and her answers were digging her deeper and deeper into a hole.

She was trying to show her beloved four year old daughter off. Why??

Another story for you: I am quite competitive in some things. And I want my child to be the best- of course I do. I don't want them to get a medal for turning up. I want them to win.

So when Zara was three years old, we attended her sports day in nursery. The year before that, she was competing in the race and was winning but decided to wait for her friends to catch up. I can assure you that she got a serious lecture about winning. Yeah, yeah how lovely and how nice of her to wait for her friends, but it meant she didn't win!

So at age three, her dad and I had lectured her on leaving everyone behind and giving them a hug after the race. I had arrived before Simon and I was being a grown up like the other parents. She was doing well and I was joining in with the oohs and aahs about cute all the kids were. Then Simon arrived just in time to see Zara win the race. From the back of the crowd I could hear him whooping and shouting "YES!! THAT IS MY GIRL! YES!!" I wish I was able to signal him to calm it down a bit... he was making it too much about winning. I was doing the same, but quietly. I felt sorry for the parents standing next to Simon whose children were not acting on instructions to "win or don't come home". We were joking, but we sort of meant it. (Monkey covering face emoji).

Don't feel bad for being proud of your children. Just don't be insensitive. Also, don't let someone's bragging make you feel inadequate as a parent.

I was so guilty of this. Other children doing stuff that mine hadn't done or couldn't do made me feel like a failure. I am in so many mummy groups online and luckily, I have outgrown the shame that I used to feel when my child didn't seem to measure up.

You find yourself obsessing about another person's child and following their progress and trying to bend your child into someone else's mold. It is soul destroying.

What I have learned to do and it is just amazing, is that I have focused on MY child. I have got to know them and I have enjoyed knowing their quirks. I have enjoyed celebrating what it is they can do. If I come across something I admire in another child, I ask myself, how important will that be in five years' time, in 10 years' time? If it won't matter, I will not stress about it. If I still fancy my child having that skill, I will ask the parent for tips.

Zara was potty trained before she was age two. Xanthe who is usually quicker to learn than Zara was four months away from her third birthday and is not cooperating with my potty-training skills. Stressed? Nope!

I am not advocating lazy parenting. I am advocating that you have compassion on yourself while you are doing your best. I am advocating that you remember to have fun and magnify your kid's strengths rather than pressure them and pressure yourself over something that really doesn't matter.

When my kids are in public, I am forever correcting them, telling them to say please, and thank you and sorry. I am always saying, no don't do that, don't say that etc etc.

I am aware that some parents think I am too strict. But there are somethings that matter to me. My culture and my upbringing demand that my children say hello when they see someone they know. It is important to me that children know how to comport themselves when they are talking to someone who is older than they are. This is because when they visit Nigeria, these are the things that count.

I have been silently proud of the fact that Zara has been able to dress herself for school since she was three years old. She is five now and I recently heard a grand dad at the school gates bragging really loudly about how good his grand daughter is at putting her socks and shoes on before school. He was so pumped, so proud. It was nice to see.

There is absolutely nothing wrong with boasting about your child's abilities. Perhaps, sometimes it is wise to pause and ask yourself why you are doing it.

Now that Zara is in proper school, I have seen the extent to which perceptions differ.

She was told to come to school with a home-made crown. I don't even remember what it was for. Simon, my mum and I went to town on this thing. We wanted Zara to be happy with it. We produced what we thought was the be all and end all of all crowns! Till we got to her school the next morning. Wow! We saw crowns of all shapes and sizes. Some people went all out. While my heart was warmed, I am aware that people saw the elaborate crowns as people trying to show off.

Another question for you is why do people's praise of their children affect you negatively? Why does it speak negatively to you?

Guilt

Prepare to feel guilty about a lot of things. Before we have children, we have these ideals in our minds. Things we would never do; things we would do; things we would never say; things we would say.

We look at other families and silently judge them for many many things.

I know for a fact that here in the UK, people judge me for working as hard and as often as I do. Sometimes, I judge myself. But I know what life I am trying to create for my children. They are not deprived of quality time with me. I find that it is women who do not work or who work only part time who judge me. The thing is, I judge them too. In my eyes, why are they not teaching their children proper work ethic?

The truth is that, by working part time, they are not teaching their children the wrong work ethic and by me working full time, I am not neglecting my children. We have different reasons for the choices we make and at the time we are making those decisions, we genuinely believe that they are what is best for our families. We are only doing what we believe is best.

There are times however, where the demands of my career has caused me to spend less time than I would like.

There are times that I am not able to provide everything that I know my children need or should have.

Not so long ago, Zara's school shoes were in desperate need to be changed. Walking with her to school and seeing her struggle with it was a lot. I knew I would be able to change them come pay day, but for the week that she had to cope with them, it was difficult to watch.

Recently, Simon broke his ankle while skateboarding (side eye emoji). We had booked our first family holiday that did not involve visiting family. We had some money and we could go on this holiday that was much needed. Because of Simon's accident, we had to cancel the holiday. Because he could not work, it affected his earnings and the whole situation had far reaching consequences for all of us. Zara asked almost on daily basis when we would be able to go on that holiday.

It was so difficult to explain to her. She had told her friends and she was extremely excited! We had made so many plans.

This is a difficult thing for me to write about. There are many times I have let my kids down. Times I have been working from home and not been able to give them any attention. Times I have not been patient enough to let them talk to me. Times I have missed something to do with their health or general wellbeing.

My tip is that you need to remember that you are human. As long as you are doing your best and always letting your children know how loved they are, they will be ok.

When you make a mistake, say sorry. This is something I have learned from my parents. They say sorry. On the rare occasions they get it wrong with us, they say sorry. It makes me love them even more.

I watched Zara's face when I have said sorry to her. I can almost see her heart swell with love and compassion for me. She comes and gives me a hug and says " it is ok mummy, I am sorry too" or she says "it is ok mummy, don't worry about it". This chapter is proving harder to write than I thought it would. My children deserve the best there is. The thought of letting them down tears me apart. But I have to be realistic and accept that like all human beings, I will make mistakes.

When I make a decision that I know is unpalatable but the right thing to do, I try to explain it to them. I try to carry them along.

Someone said I talk to my children like they are adults. It was an observation I agreed with. I don't talk to them in adult terms, but I do discuss with them as much as I can. I have as many conversations as I can with them.

As they are growing, I am seeing the benefits of it. I see Zara's confidence in approaching me to talk about anything. Even if it is something she knows she may get into trouble for. She comes and tries to talk through it.

When I snap unnecessarily, on occasion, she explains to me why I have just done that. When I have to work, I don't have to explain as much anymore. She gets it.

So you will feel guilty. You know why? Because you care. Because they matter enough for you to assess your behavior towards them. They matter enough for you to sacrifice somethings now to ensure they have a future that they can thank you for.

Have Fun!

This is where I think I have a natural flare. We have many many laughs in our house. It is important to me that my children laugh. It is important that we have the rough and tumble and the carefree approach to life.

I find something to enjoy in as many moments as possible. My Facebook page is full of videos and pictures that I look at and smile.

I can't tell you how much those pictures and videos have helped my mental health. During the tough times, I scroll through our memories and it helps.

Having fun does not have to cost anything. Give your children a chance to get to know you. Not just the "mum" you, but you as a person.

When you get to that age where they are asking every question under the sun: "mummy why is that man running? Why is he running like that? Why is he wearing a green shirt? Will he get tired after running? Why is he wearing those shoes? Why are his shoes black?

Do you think he has other shoes? Why is he a man?... enjoy it.

I was getting to the point where the questions were driving me crazy! But I had to check myself. The little girl is presenting me an opportunity to be the one who speaks into her life, who shapes her reality and I am shutting her up. I don't want her going anywhere else at that age to get validation or information.

So I started getting creative with my answers. I said the first thing that popped into my head if it was one of those ridiculous questions. Sometimes my answers made me laugh out loud.

It is impossible to have a close family without in jokes.

My tip is that you should be deliberate in creating your children's memories. When I sit and reminisce with my siblings, the things that cause us to laugh the most are the in jokes; the things that weld us closer together are the memories that I now know my parents were deliberate about.

The End

I hope this hasn't come across as a lecture. I wanted to be like your friend chatting away about "her" stuff. It is not an academic thesis. It is not a manual on anything. I am no expert. I am just a girl who became a mum.

I doubt I have said anything profound. I don't think I have said anything you do not already know.

Hopefully it was just a reminder that being a parent is about you and your child. It is about the path that you map out together. By all means look for answers to the issues your children present you with. But please, don't forget to look inwards too. You know them better than anyone else in the world.

There are some solutions that only you can provide.

Thank you for reading.

Peace and love

Ije *x*

Printed in Great Britain
by Amazon